MONSTERS

CENTAURS

BY KEVIN HILE

KIDHAVEN PRESS

A part of Gale, Cengage Learning

GALE
CENGAGE Learning™

Detroit • New York • San Francisco • New Haven, Conn • Waterville, Maine • London

GALE
CENGAGE Learning‑

LIBRARY OF CONGRESS CATALOGING-IN-PUBLICATION DATA

Hile, Kevin.
  Centaurs / by Kevin Hile.
    p. cm. — (Monsters)
  Includes bibliographical references and index.
  ISBN 978-0-7377-4042-4 (hardcover)
  1. Centaurs—Juvenile literature. I. Title.
  BL820.C37H55 2008
  398'.45—dc22

                                                        2008008759

KidHaven Press
27500 Drake Rd.
Farmington Hills, MI 48331

ISBN-13: 978-0-7377-4042-4
ISBN-10: 0-7377-4042-6

Printed in the United States of America
2 3 4 5 6 7 12 11 10 09 08

CONTENTS

CHAPTER 1

HALF MAN, HALF HORSE

Many of the mythological creatures that are well known today began in ancient Greece. Greek civilization roughly spanned the years from 750 B.C. to 146 B.C., when the Greeks were conquered by the Roman Empire. During these centuries, the Greeks had a rich culture that included art, grand buildings and temples, and many stories of gods and fantastic creatures. One of these creatures was the centaur.

A centaur is a mix between a human and a horse. The centaur that most people are familiar with has a human head, arms, and torso attached to a horse's body where the horse's head would be. The bottom half of the centaur includes the horse's body, four legs, and a tail. But this is not the only version of the centaur.

Originally, the centaur was a kind of demon called a *kallikantzaroi*. It looked like a human being from head to foot, but it had the torso and back legs of a horse sticking out from its back. In other words, the first centaurs stood on four feet. The front feet were human feet, and the back feet were those of a horse.

Being half horse, half man, the centaur had the strength of a wild animal and the intelligence of a person. This made it a tough opponent in battle.

The centaur that most people are familiar with is a mix between a human and a horse.

Versions of the Centaur

The idea of a half-human, half-animal creature was not unique to the Greeks. It was common in many ancient cultures.

The ancient Sumerians, who lived about 5,000 years ago in what is now Iraq, told stories of a creature named Hes Bani who was part bull. Hes Bani was famous for his wisdom. The Mesopotamians, who also lived in the area of modern Iraq, had a centaur like creature in their mythology, too. It was called the urmahlullu. The urmahlullu had the body and legs of a lion, however, instead of those of a horse.

In Arabic cultures there is the story of Al Borak, a creature with the face of a man—except the cheeks were those of a horse—the body of a horse, the wings of an eagle, and feathers like those of a peacock. Al Borak was given to the prophet Muhammad by the angel Gabriel. Muhammad was then able to ride Al Borak to visit the Seven Heavens in a trip called the Miraj. It was a simple task for the wondrous centaur, who could make the trip in a single stride.

Another culture that told stories of centaurs, the Scythians, settled in the lands north of Iran around the time of the ancient Greeks. The Scythian version of the centaur was called an onocentaur. Onocentaurs had the upper body of a human and the lower body of a donkey.

Centaurs

Half-human, half-animal creatures were common in ancient times. The Mesopotamians had a creature called the urmahlullu, which had the body and legs of a lion.

The Romans also had stories of centaurs, but these were taken from the Greek myths. The Romans adapted many of these stories to their own culture.

Origins in Thessaly

The Greek centaur is the one most familiar to Americans. It is possible that the Greeks' idea of the centaur came from an outside culture, such as the Scythians. Many **archaeologists** think it is more likely that the Greeks formed the myth after encountering the Thessalonian (*theh-suh-loh-nyuhn*) culture (sometimes called Thessalian) in a remote forested region of what is now modern Greece.

In those days, horses were not in common use in Greece, having arrived in that region around the year 2000 B.C. The people in Thessaly were among the first to master them. They are credited, too, with having invented the bit (the mouthpiece of a bridle worn on a horse's head).

One theory about the origin of the centaur myth, then, is that the Greeks encountered the Thessalonians as they were riding horses and possibly mistook them for half-human, half-horse animals. (Much later, in the 16th century, the Mayans

Some archaeologists think that the Greeks came up with their version of the centaur after witnessing the Thessalonians riding horses. The Thessalonians were known for their horse breeding and equestrian skills.

Centaurs

and Incans of Central and South America would make the same mistake when Spanish conquerors arrived in their lands.)

Another possibility is that the early Greeks witnessed the Thessalonians practicing a kind of religious ritual. Archaeologists know that the Thessalonians worshipped the horse in an unusual way. During religious rituals Thessalonians strapped objects to their rears that were made to look like the rear ends of horses. The people of Thessaly were noted hunters, too, and they were called the "bull killers" by the Greeks because it was their custom to hunt bulls while on horseback. In the Greek language, "bull killer" is *kentauroi,* which is what the tribe came to be called. This word was later changed by Latin speakers of Rome to *centauri,* and, in English, *centaurs.*

Entering the Mythology

Once the idea of a half-horse human entered the imaginations of the ancient Greeks, it was only a matter of time before centaurs became part of their mythology. The Greeks were great storytellers, and they created a complex world populated by many gods and magical creatures. These myths began as **oral traditions**. They typically begin not as written stories, but as stories that are spoken, passed from person to person. In this way, many versions of a tale can emerge, which is true of the story of centaurs. The story of how centaurs were created varies, depending on the origin of the tale.

According to one myth, the centaurs descended from a king named Ixion. Ixion ruled a group of people called the Lapiths in Thessaly and was guilty of great crimes. He married the daughter of Deioneus, but Ixion did not pay his father-in-law the bride price he promised. To get back at Ixion, Deioneus stole some of Ixion's horses. Ixion then got revenge on Deioneus by killing him. For this murder, Ixion was punished and exiled, or sent away. Ixion's crimes were so serious that no other tribe would accept him. Zeus, the king of the gods, pitied Ixion and allowed the former king to visit Olympus, the land of the gods.

While in Olympus, Ixion fell in love with Zeus's wife, Hera. When Zeus found out Ixion was pursuing Hera, he decided to trick Ixion by making a copy of Hera out of a cloud. He named the cloud Nephele. Ixion fell in love with Nephele, thinking it was Hera. The two had a child—Centaurus. Zeus further punished Ixion by having him tied to a wheel of fire, which would spin for eternity.

CENTAURUS

Meanwhile, Ixion and Nephele's son, Centaurus, lived on Mount Pelion. In Greek mythology there are many stories in which gods and humans fell in love with and had babies with animals. They believed that such unions could result in creatures that were part human and part animal, such as minotaurs (half human, half bull). This was the case

According to Greek mythology, the centaurs were descendants of Ixion, a king. Ixion fell in love with Zeus's wife and, as punishment, Zeus tied him to a wheel, which spun for eternity.

with Centaurus. According to one myth, Centaurus and the mares of Magnesia are the parents of the race of creatures called centaurs.

In another version of the centaur myth the father of the centaur race is not Centaurus but Ixion. Nephele gives birth to the centaurs herself. In yet

In Greek mythology, there are many versions of the centaur myth and of Centaurus.

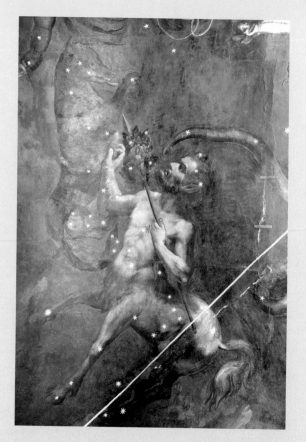

another story, Zeus and Ixion's wife, Dia, are the centaurs' parents.

Still other sources from Greek times provide other explanations for the centaurs. One has them arising from a cloud, not coming from parents. In yet another version of the story, Centaurus was born of the god Apollo and Stilbe, the daughter of a river god. Some stories say Centaurus had a twin brother named Lapithes. Centaurus was the father of the centaurs, and Lapithes founded the tribe called the Lapiths.

CHAPTER 2

FROM ENEMIES TO FRIENDS

Once centaurs entered into the mythology of the Greeks, a number of stories were told about them. The first centaurs were seen as rough creatures that could become violent and dangerous, especially when they drank wine. Over time, however, the Greeks wrote tales about more friendly centaurs. Some centaurs even had admirable skills. They were described as talented **archers** who were allies to the Greeks in important battles. One famous centaur, Chiron, was even said to be the founder of medicine. He was also a philosopher and teacher to some Greek heroes.

BATTLE WITH THE LAPITHS

The most famous early story about aggressive centaurs is their battle against the Lapiths. King Pirithous, the leader of the Lapiths, planned to marry Hippodamia, whose name means "tamer of horses." The king invited not only his fellow tribespeople to the wedding, but also those who were related to the Lapiths, including the centaurs.

Wine was served as part of the celebration. However, the centaurs did not normally drink wine, so they quickly became drunk. This caused them to be aggressive. One of the centaurs, Eurytion, saw the beautiful Hippodamia and tried to attack her. The Greek hero Theseus immediately came to Hippo-

Another Greek myth talks about aggressive centaurs and their battle with the Lapiths.

damia's aid. Soon, all the centaurs and men were fighting each other in a horrible battle.

Theseus caught Eurytion and, as punishment, cut off his nose and ears. The centaurs lost the battle, and they were banished from Thessaly. The centaurs fled to Mount Pholoe, where they settled.

Myths are often used as ways to impart lessons, and the story of the centaurs and Lapiths is no exception. In this case, it is an example of the potential dangers of drinking too much wine. The battle is also a **symbol** of the conflict between humans and beasts, or between civilization and untamed nature.

THE STORY OF NESSUS AND HERCULES

Many other Greek myths include centaurs as characters. They usually appear as secondary characters in myths about famous Greek heroes such as Hercules (known to the Greeks as Heracles), Achilles, and Jason. Sometimes, the centaurs are good people, and other times they are bad.

One very tragic tale is about Hercules and the centaur Nessus. The hero Hercules traveled to the city of Calydon. There he met Deianira, the daughter of King Oeneus. Hercules saved Deianira from the river god Achelous, who wanted her for his own and tried to kidnap her. Achelous tried to take Deianira while in the form of a dragon, a bull, and a river, but Hercules rescued Deianira and married her. Living with his new wife and son in Calydon, Hercules did a foolish thing: He got angry and, without meaning to, killed an innocent man with his godlike strength.

Hercules took his family and fled the city in fear. On their way, they came to the Evenus River. They needed to get across, because the king was chasing them. Hercules was strong enough to swim the river, but his wife needed help. The centaur Nessus offered to carry her, but as they were crossing, the centaur found Deianira so delightful that he wanted her for himself. The jealous Hercules shot him with an arrow.

Before the centaur died, though, he told Deianira a secret. If she collected some of his blood, she could use it as a love potion, just in case her husband later became attracted to another woman. Deianira, however, did not realize that Nessus's blood would be a poison to Hercules.

Of course, there would be no story if Deianira ignored the centaur. She did as Nessus suggested, and, sure enough, Hercules later fell in love with a woman named Iole. Desperately wanting her husband back,

Deianira used the centaur's blood. She put some of it on a shirt and gave it to Hercules. When the hero put the shirt on, the blood in the shirt killed Hercules. Stricken with grief because she had never wanted to kill her husband, Deianira committed suicide. Fortunately for Hercules, he was the son of Zeus, and Zeus granted him immortality.

The story of Hercules, Deianira, and the centaur Nessus is a tragic Greek myth in which Nessus does a bad deed.

Chiron, the Kindly Centaur

Not all centaurs in Greek mythology are guilty of bad deeds. One centaur in particular stands out as a noble and helpful person: Chiron. Chiron (sometimes spelled Cheiron), in some versions of the myth, was the son of Cronus (or Saturn, in Roman mythology). Cronus was a Titan god who was also the father of Zeus, among other gods. In this way, Chiron was different from the other centaurs. He was not a son of Centaurus or Ixion. He looked like other centaurs, however, because Cronus had taken on the form of a horse when he was with Chiron's mother, Philyria.

As a son of the gods, Chiron was an immortal. He was also different from the other centaurs in that he was much more civilized. Rejected by his father, Chiron was educated by the gods Artemis and Apollo, so he did not follow the more barbaric ways of the other centaurs.

Apollo was the god of music and poetry, as well as of healing, prophecy (predicting the future), and archery, all of which he taught to Chiron. Artemis, Apollo's twin sister, was the goddess of the hunt. She, too, was familiar with the bow and arrow. Like her brother, she was a lover of music, dance, and poetry, but she had a dark side. Artemis was also a goddess of death.

Chiron lived on Mount Pelion in Thessaly. After receiving his education, he too became a teacher.

He taught such heroes as Hercules, Jason, Achilles (as well as Achilles' father, Peleus), Aeneas, and Asclepius. It was Asclepius who took over the role of god of medicine and healing after Chiron's death.

Chiron was different from other centaurs. He was noble and civilized and became a teacher, where he taught heroes such as Achilles about art and music.

The Deaths of Chiron and Pholus

The tale of Chiron's death is another tragic story. Hercules, Chiron's friend and student, was known for killing a number of the more barbaric centaurs who inhabited Thessaly. One day, during a battle against the centaurs, Hercules was shooting arrows that contained the poisonous blood of the monstrous serpent called the Hydra. During the heat of battle, Hercules accidentally wounded Chiron with one of these arrows.

But Chiron was immortal, so the poison could not kill him. Nevertheless, it caused him great agony that could never be relieved. The centaur suffered for a long time, but then Zeus took pity on him. He allowed Chiron to transfer his immortal powers to Prometheus, the god known for giving the gift of fire to humans.

With his burden of immortality removed, Chiron finally died. But he found immortality in another way when Zeus created the **constellation** Sagittarius in Chiron's image.

Along with Chiron, another famous centaur died as a result of Hercules' arrow: Pholus. Pholus was a friend to Hercules and was considered another wise centaur. Like Chiron, Pholus was not descended from Centaurus. Instead, he was the son of a satyr named Silenus. After the battle in which Hercules used his poisoned arrows, Pholus was examining one of the poisoned tips and accidentally

Both Chiron and Pholus died or were wounded accidently from Hercules' poisonous arrow.

dropped it on his foot. The poison from the arrow-head killed him immediately.

When Pholus died, Hercules buried his friend at the base of the mountain named after the centaur: Mount Pholoe. Today that mountain in Greece is known as Mount Pholois.

Centaurs

CHAPTER 3

SURVIVING THE AGES

Greek civilization fell into decline by the second century B.C. A new power in Europe had arisen by that time–the Roman Empire. Over a period of years, they conquered Greece and made it part of their empire. The Romans not only took political command of Greece, they also adopted the Greek culture, including its mythology. They often changed the names of the Greek gods and heroes as they worked them into Roman stories. Zeus became Jupiter and Heracles became Hercules, for example. But the stories remained essentially the same, and centaurs remained centaurs.

The stories of centaurs continued for several centuries, surviving in Roman myths. Then, in A.D. 476, the Roman civilization in Western Europe collapsed. Europe was overtaken by various tribes such as the Visigoths, Franks, and Alemanni.

For the next 800 years (often called the **Dark Ages**), the tales of the centaurs were largely forgotten in Europe. But sometimes a lord would use the image of a centaur on his **coat of arms**. These were symbols that leaders put on flags or battle shields to represent their royal families. The most famous person to have a centaur on his coat of arms was King Stephen of England, who ruled that country in the 12th century. The symbol of the centaur represented strength, wisdom, and military skill.

Centaurs were also remembered in the constellations.

CENTAURS IN ASTROLOGY

Ancient cultures believed that the stars and planets, and their movements through the heavens, had an influence on people's lives. Indeed, many people today still believe they can predict what will happen to people by studying the stars. This is called **astrology**.

The Greeks believed that the father of the centaurs, Centaurus, taught people to read the signs in the stars and organized the stars into their present constellations. When people looked up into the sky, the arrangement of the stars formed pictures in their minds, such as lions, scorpions, and fish. Twelve of these constellations are called the signs of the Zodiac, and one

of those signs is Sagittarius. Also known as the Archer, Sagittarius is the constellation that represents a centaur archer in the sky. Many people think this centaur represents Chiron.

People born under the sign of Sagittarius (November 22 to December 21) are said to possess both animal and human traits. They are both very physical and very intelligent people. The archery symbol in Sagittarius is seen as both a good and bad quality. It

Sagittarius, a constellation and one of the twelve Zodiac signs, represents a centaur archer in the sky.

can mean that Sagittarians are heroic and bold people of action, or it could mean that they may be impulsive, may be too quick to act, and can miss their mark.

But Sagittarius is not the only constellation that honors a centaur. The other is Centaurus, which some people say honors Chiron and others say Pholus. Still others logically conclude that the constellation is named after Centaurus, the father of the centaurs.

Revival in the Renaissance

By the 14th century, Europe had begun to recover from the Dark Ages and enter a period of history known as the **Renaissance**. This period in history saw the formation of more stable governments and a renewed interest in the arts. People started looking back on the classical age of Greece and Rome for inspiration in architecture, painting, and literature.

Many artists put centaurs into their artwork. They often depicted stories from the **classical period** that helped keep the stories of centaurs alive. For example, the battle between the Lapiths and centaurs is depicted in a 15th-century painting by Piero di Cosimo (1462–1522). Michelangelo was another, even more famous artist of the era who used centaurs in his work. His *Battle of the Centaurs* (1492) is a marble carving that depicts centaurs at war. Scholars are unsure, though, whether it is sup-

posed to represent the battle against the Lapiths or perhaps centaurs fighting Hercules.

Artistic interest in centaurs continued over the next several centuries or so in Europe, occasionally being revived with new archaeological discoveries. For instance, in 1736 Monsignor Giuseppe Alessandro Furietti discovered two Roman statues of centaurs. Dating from the time of Roman emperor

Michelangelo was one of many artists who used centaurs in their artwork. His marble relief, Battle of the Centaurs, *depicts the centaurs at war.*

Hadrian (A.D. 76–138), the perfectly preserved statues became known as the Furietti Centaurs. One is a statue of a young male centaur, and the other is of an old centaur. The centaur statues inspired many artists at the time, who used these Roman pieces as models for their own artwork.

LITERATURE AND CENTAURS

Centaurs appeared not only in many artistic works since the Renaissance but also in literature. As with artists such as Michelangelo, poets and other authors often looked back to classical Greece and

Centaurs also appear in literature. William Shakespeare used a violent centaur in Titus Andronicus. *In his play, a centaur cuts off the hands of Lavinia.*

Rome for their inspiration. Sometimes they depicted centaurs negatively.

For example, in two plays by William Shakespeare (1564–1616)–*A Midsummer Night's Dream* and *Titus Andronicus*–centaurs are characters who are either violent or have bad reputations. *Titus Andronicus* has a centaur that cuts off the hands of a woman named Lavinia. In *A Midsummer Night's Dream*, Shakespeare refers to the centaurs' battle with the Lapiths. Another famous person from Shakespeare's time, the philosopher Thomas Hobbes (1588–1679), used centaurs in his book *Leviathan* to represent people who lacked intelligence.

Part of the reason behind the unfavorable view of centaurs was the influence of Christian beliefs. In Europe, the typical Christian saw the image of the half-horse, half-man centaur as something unholy and evil. Poets such as Edmund Spenser (c. 1552–1599) described centaurs as barbaric. In Spenser's *The Faerie Queen*, for example, the poet describes them as being dreadful.

By the 1700s, however, artists' views of centaurs became kinder, even romantic. More and more, writers viewed centaurs in the positive image created by Chiron–as teachers, archers, and friends. Matthew Arnold (1822–1888) wrote about Chiron in his poetry collection, *Empedocles on Etna*, as a wise teacher. The centaurs' addiction to wine, though, was still mentioned in this work. The Romantic era poet John Keats (1795–1821) praised the archery skills of centaurs in a poem called *Endymion.*

The admiring view of centaurs continued to appear in writing into the 20th and 21st centuries, as centaurs became popular creatures in the styles of writing called science fiction and fantasy.

CHAPTER 4

CENTAURS IN SPACE AND FANTASY

By the 1950s, people were becoming more hopeful that one day humans would travel to other planets and possibly discover aliens.

SCIENCE FICTION CHARACTERS

The idea of space travel was exciting the imaginations of authors. A new type of literature called science fiction gained popularity. Some science fiction writers drew on characters from mythology to create stories of alien centaurs.

Sometimes centaur characters in science fiction appear only briefly, such as in Madeleine L'Engle's (1918–2007) classic *A Wrinkle in Time* (1962). In other novels they are feature characters. Author

John Varley (1947–), for example, includes a centaur race in his Gaea trilogy, which includes *Titan* (1979), *Wizard* (1980), and *Demon* (1984). In these stories, space travelers arrive on a living planet ruled by a female, godlike being who creates races of people based on her knowledge of Earth. One of these races is the centaurs. The centaur characters in Varley's book are highly intelligent and often kind, but they also can be dangerous warriors.

Another popular science fiction series with centaurs is the Well World series by Jack L. Chalker (1944–2005). The first book, *Midnight at the Well of Souls* (1977), introduces readers to Nathan Brazil, a starship captain who lands on the Well World. This strange place features all kinds of creatures, including centaurs. The human characters often find themselves turned into these creatures. Nathan himself is turned into a centaur in *The Return of Nathan Brazil* (1979).

In these and other science fiction tales, centaurs are typically shown as aliens who happen to resemble the mythical creatures of Greece. Other than that, they usually have nothing in common with the classic tales.

CENTAURS IN OUTER SPACE

As telescopes improved, scientists discovered new outer space objects. Among these objects is a belt of **planetoids**, or large asteroids, located between

the orbits of the planets Jupiter and Neptune. They were first identified in the late 1970s, and astronomers called them "the centaurs."

The first "centaur" was found in 1977 and named Chiron. Because Chiron has a tail, it is now

Chiron is a large asteroid that orbits the sun. Astronomers called these large asteroids "the centaurs."

considered a comet and not a planetoid. Two other centaurs called 60558 Echeclus and 166P/NEAT 2001 T4 are now classified as comets, too. The famous centaurs Nessus and Pholus also have planetoids named after them in the centaur belt.

THE RISE OF FANTASY

About the same time that science fiction stories became popular, fantasy fiction also found an audience. British author J.R.R. Tolkien (1892–1973) is credited with inspiring the modern type of fantasy books. Tolkien's The Lord of the Rings series of books feature wizards, dwarfs, elves, and little people called hobbits. Centaurs are mentioned briefly in Tolkien's fiction, but he sparked the imaginations of others to create new worlds filled with centaurs and other mythical beasts.

One such author was Tolkien's friend C.S. Lewis (1898–1963). Lewis's most beloved series of books, The Chronicles of Narnia, is made up of seven books published from 1950 to 1956.

Lewis did not have a negative view of centaurs as beasts and brutes. Instead, he modeled his centaurs more in the image of Chiron. They are noble and brave creatures that

are talented archers and good at military strategy. They fight at the side of Aslan, the lion king whose armies fight off the evil hordes attacking Narnia.

Lewis's centaurs are also wise, and they are skilled at reading the movements of the stars and planets. Part of their wisdom, too, comes from living for a long time. In The Chronicles of Narnia,

C.S. Lewis portrays centaurs as noble and brave creatures in his series of books, The Chronicles of Narnia. The Chronicles of Narnia: The Lion, the Witch and the Wardrobe *was made into a film in 2005.*

some centaurs are more than 500 years old. Lewis does not forget the old stories of centaurs and wine, but in his stories he says that their large horse stomachs allow them to drink a lot of wine without losing their senses. One of the centaur characters, Cloudbirth, is also a healer, just like Chiron. Other centaurs in the books, such as Roonwit and Glenstorm, are friends to the English children who arrive in Narnia and help save it.

HUMOROUS AND POPULAR CENTAURS

Some modern fantasy authors have taken a humorous view of centaurs and other magical creatures. The Xanth books (1977–2005) by Piers Anthony (1934–) are fantasy stories full of puns and jokes. Anthony creates a complicated family of centaur characters in his Xanth world, a place where everyone has a unique magical talent. For example, Chet Centaur has the ability to make any object small. The only problem, however, is that he cannot make them big again. This flaw provides a lot of humor in the stories. Anthony's centaurs are characters with human qualities, with both strong and weak points. The author even uses some centaurs as main characters in his novels. One is named Cheiron, in honor of the Greek centaur.

One of the most popular fantasy series of all time, the Harry Potter books by J.K. Rowling (1965–), includes centaurs as well. Rowling views centaurs as astrologers, philosophers, healers,

archers, and teachers. Young Harry first meets a centaur named Firenze in *Harry Potter and the Sorcerer's Stone* (1997).

Many modern fantasy tales have centaur characters. In Harry Potter and the Sorcerer's Stone, *Harry meets a centaur named Firenze.*

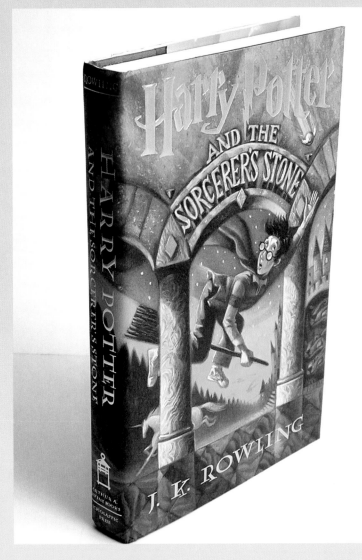

Firenze, who only makes a brief appearance in the first book in the series, proves to be an unusual centaur. Appearing again in later Harry Potter books, Firenze seems to like humans, while his fel-

Centaurs often appear in comic books, graphic novels, fantasy art, and games.

low centaurs stay away from them. In fact, when Firenze becomes a teacher at the Hogwarts school, the other centaurs banish him. Firenze is accepted back into the centaur herd only after he helps win the battle against the evil Voldemort in *Harry Potter and the Deathly Hallows* (2007).

COMIC BOOKS, FANTASY ART, AND GAMES

Centaurs are also sometimes portrayed in movies, such as the film versions of the Harry Potter books. A number of comic books—and, more recently, graphic novels—have included centaurs, too. Among the popular comic book series that have included centaurs are Superman, Captain Marvel, Metal Men, Avengers, Micronauts, Scary Tales, and Arak.

A side effect of fantasy literature's popularity has been the appearance of centaurs in fantasy art and games. A famous artist named Boris Vallejo has painted numerous pictures of centaurs, often for use as fantasy book covers or for calendars. These paintings tend to emphasize the power, exotic beauty, and warrior qualities of the centaur.

Fantasy video and card games also tend to portray centaurs as warriors, usually dangerous ones. In games such as Dungeons and Dragons and Magic: The Gathering, players face creatures such as centaurs as they compete against each other. Dangerous centaurs also appear in video games such as Tomb Raider and Mortal Kombat. Mortal Kombat is particularly inventive with its centaurs.

Called "Centaurians" in the game, they can be combinations of human forms with either horses, bulls, rams, goats, or even reptilian creatures.

Whether they are friends or foes, centaurs of the past and present remain an imaginative creation from ancient history that live on to this day.

GLOSSARY

archaeologist: A person who studies peoples and cultures of ancient civilizations.

archer/archery: A person who hunts or fights using a bow and arrows; the practice of using bows and arrows.

astrology: The practice of studying the movements of planets and stars in order to make predictions about the future.

classical period: A general term that refers to the centuries in which the Greeks and Romans thrived.

coat of arms: Unique symbols used by a knight or a royal person to identify his or her family and land of origin.

constellation: Any collection of stars that are grouped together and have been given a unique name.

Dark Ages: Often called the Middle Ages, this is the time between the fall of the Roman Empire and the beginning of the Renaissance in Europe—roughly between the 5th and 14th centuries.

oral tradition: The practice of passing down stories and histories from generation to generation verbally, rather than in writing.

planetoids: Sometimes referred to as asteroids, planetoids are space objects that are smaller than a planet or moon.

Renaissance: The period in European history from about the 1300s through the 1600s that was marked by a renewed interest in science and culture.

symbol: A thing that represents another thing.

FOR FURTHER EXPLORATION

BOOKS

Thomas Bulfinch. *Bulfinch's Mythology*. New York: Modern Library, 2004. This classic source for studying Greek mythology summarizes the myths. An introduction explains the Greek gods and goddesses and their various domains.

Kathleen N. Daly. *Greek & Roman Mythology A to Z*. New York: Facts On File, 2004. Alphabetically arranged entries on topics in Greek and Roman Mythology aimed at middle school readers.

Anne Pearson. *Ancient Greece*. New York: DK, 2004. A highly illustrated overview of Ancient Greek culture.

WEB SITES

Theoi Greek Mythology, "Kentauroi Thessalioi" (www.theoi.com/Georgikos/Kentauroi Thessalioi. html). A great overview of the mythology of the centaurs, including many excerpts from texts by Ovid, Homer, and other classic Greek authors who mention centaurs in their writings.

INDEX

PICTURE CREDITS

ABOUT THE AUTHOR

Kevin Hile is a freelance writer, editor, and Web site designer based in Michigan. A graduate of Adrian College, where he met his wife, Janet, he has been a reference book editor for almost twenty years. Hile is a former Detroit Zoo volunteer who is currently a docent and Web site manager for the Potter Park Zoo in Lansing. Deeply concerned about the environment, animals, and wildlife conservation, he is also the author of *Animal Rights* (Chelsea House, 2004) and *Little Zoo by the Red Cedar* (MSU Press, 2008). Hile is a regular contributor to Gale's Contemporary Authors series. He is also the author of *Dams and Levees* for KidHaven Press.